A Peace of My Mind

What People are Saying About A Peace of My Mind!

"It's a **nostalgic phenomenon** that takes you back to Kool-aid, cornrows and REAL black love." **Shawnika Anderson**

"...it's a **living, breathing collection** of poetry. **I found myself** in it, many times." **Charlagne Ferguson**

"....at times, I found A Peace of My Mind to **invoke sweet memories.** In many places it is very sensual and its full of subtle wisdom." **Whitney Mack**

"Vickie is a **gifted and talented** young woman. I look forward to more reads from her." **Amy Hooper-Johnson**

"It's **sultry, mesmerizing** and nostalgic. This book is REAL" **Tiedra Hutchings**

" Very **clever and innovative**... great book. Can't wait for the next one." **Christopher Carodine**

A Peace of My Mind is **thought provoking**. It's a good read for girlfriends." **Tracy Dillingham (TracyfromCincinatti)**

"**I love the book and loved the Book Signing Event!** reading the poems and going back in time to feel those memories was heightened by hearing those words from the voice of the author... a confirmation that i did indeed - get it!"
Darlene Dickson of Manifold Grace Publishing House

A Peace of My Mind is a **candid, soul-filled anthology** of poetic experiences that is relative to every facet of African-American life."
Dr. Natasha Woody

A Peace of My Mind

Vickie Brent-Touray

The Baobab Press, LLC
Marietta, Georgia

2014

A Peace of My Mind

by Vickie Brent-Touray

ed. Malou Cristobal

Published in the United States by

The Baobab Press, LLC

www.thebaobabpress.com

(The "Bow Bow" Press)

Marietta, GA

ISBN: 9780989375719

Cover Design:
Perfecting Image Photgraphy and Designs
Redford, MI

For You

For you, who I truly believe was guided in my direction by the Almighty for a purpose that was much greater than you and I.

For you, who has been my sounding board, my encouragement, my voice of reason, when I couldn't see the light of day.

For you, who wrapped your thoughts and prayers around me when we weren't able to take each other by the hand.

For you, who listened to all my dreams and visions and chanted "Team Vickie! Team Vickie B! Team Touray!

For **Kire Senoj**, who asked me every time we spoke-- sarcastically, "So...when are you going to publish that book?" Thank you Brother, you've been that "iron" that sharpens iron.

For **Dr. Chris Tysh** of Wayne State University, who told me more times than a few, that I should "do something" with my writing.

For **Dr. Eugenia Shittu** of Wilberforce University, who kept me on track, mentored me, encouraged me--focused me, in the right direction when I forgot why I had gone to Wilberforce University (tee hee).

For **Mrs. Lorene Phillips** of Pontiac Central High School, **Home of the Mighty, Marching C-H-I-E-F-S,** who wielded her impeccable Afro and anthologies of African-American writers like a mighty sword and she sliced deep into my soul with both.

For Mrs. **Diane Butts (Jackson)**, my 5th Grade Language Arts Teacher, who was a REAL Teacher. Mrs. Butts loved on us, scolded us and reminded us everyday, of what she expected-- as well what our parents expected from us. When she finished with all that, she made sure that we could read, write *and* think. I hope I've made you proud.

I am forever grateful to you all. You all have made this thing called "life" much easier to navigate and I love you for it. I sho'nuff love you for it.

---

and especially for you...

For you, my personal "box of chocolates," I'm not sure what I did to deserve soooo much sugar, but I sure am glad I did it. My heart is yours. In the words of my littlest chocolate, "I'm so glad I found you."

All my love from here to infinity,
Your Caramel Center

For Mama and Daddy, I hope I've made you proud, I'm sho'nuff missing you.

Contents

Empowerment

Musings

About the Author...

A "70s child," Vickie Brent-Touray was born and raised about 25 miles north of Detroit in the City of Pontiac, Michigan in the wake of "great industry, greater music, the best food and even better times." The entire Midwest was thriving and pulsing in the cradle of what was affectionately called "The Big 3" (Ford, General Motors, Chrysler). It was in the cradle of this great metropolis that the author was first inspired to pen personal experiences of visions, smells and sounds that she considered truly "marvelous" on their own. Vickie Brent-Touray is a mother, wife and an educator. She currently resides in Atlanta, Georgia.

Foreword

When you think of poetry, you might think of lines that rhyme: Roses are red, violets are blue... That is not what you are going to get from this book. Get your coffees, get your lattes, get a glass of your favorite wine because you're going on a ride back to your past and deliberately into your future! Vickie is certainly going to give you the "Peace" and *a piece* of her mind- but you had better get ready.

A Peace of My Mind is filled with pieces that made me want to read them more than once. I wanted to get the full gist of everything that was going on in these pages. I'm not saying the poems are complicated or hard to understand, but while reading them, I found myself transported to a specific times in place and space. I'd often reread so that I could savor certain words and phrases to keep me in certain, "mental spaces", until I was good and ready to leave.

This book is divided into four chapters: Passion, Community, Empowerment, and Musings, of which Empowerment is my favorite. Each piece in the Empowerment chapter is no holds barred! It is like Vickie is saying "I have got to get in your face and tell you like it REALLY is." I was certainly empowered after reading this section. If you are not challenged AND uplifted after reading the pieces in this section, then you should go back and read them again, because you have certainly missed something. My favorite is "The Color Black." At some point in life, most people of color, have experienced a bout of insecurity concerning who we are and how we "fit in" as it relates to race. Whether we've tried to fit in amongst our own or others, many people of color have experienced this insecurity. This poem speaks directtly to the possibility of that insecurity. It is Empowering.

I met Vickie in 1988; fall semester to be exact. Vickie was Brent then, not Touray. Vickie was the very first person that I met as a young, "green" freshman at our beloved "Good Old WU," Wilberforce University. She's still my best friend and Sistah Gurl to this day. Although I was fiercely religious, I had never heard of John P. Kee until I met her. She was blasting John from her Boom Box like others were blasting Rob Base. She was marching to her own beat, even then.

Since then, nothing Vickie has committed to doing, including writing this book, has surprised me. From falling in and out of love, to getting a Master's degree, to traveling internationally, to marrying an international man and even becoming a mother, Vickie has done it all with greatness and also without fear [that you know of].

Even though we live 8 hours apart, I have watched her ride success like an eagle soaring on a nice summer day. Unfortunately, there were dark days as well, but that didn't break her. In our college days, we both dated a "Brother Black." Thankfully we matured and married a "Manly Man." Lord Jesus, don't let us have a flashback on "Brother Black."

While both of us are happily married, employed, and have two girls, four boys and two houses between us, you shouldn't be mistaken, we at times are both still "Disgruntled Domestics!" Wifey this, Mommy that. Buy this, buy that, take me here, help me with this, "Who's gonna help us?" This is oftentimes one of our discussion topics whenever we can "steal" a minute.

I must say I love the fact that my Gurl is naturally compassionate, most of all. A perfect example of that can be seen in her piece "A Prayer for God's Displaced Children." This poem is a true testament to her commitment to the children she teaches, mentors and nurtures as a Teacher.

This book is *right on time* for me personally, because it forces me to look at why "I'm Inside Myself" coupled with my problem "On Being Transparent Today." Sometimes it's difficult for me be transparent, but this book gets me one step closer to working through that hang up.

Help me applaud MY Sistah, MY Gurl, as she "eases on down the road" in pursuit of her success. Vickie…may the hammer of success knock the hell out of you!

W.W.A.T. for life!

Love You Gurl!

Tracy from Cincinnati

Dreadlock Prince

Who carved your ebony eyes
dark
constant
strong?
And who used the same to chisel your neck,
thick
braced
long?

On what palette can I
find your paint of
brown sugared hues?

Of what liquors do I taste
when offering my lips to you?
Is it a buttered rum?
A cognac?
Or maybe your mango wine?
Of this I have drank shamelessly,
while not at all refined.

Say to me your sweet words
The River Nile has less calm.
Make to me your promises
With every word your balm...

Come now girl, you stay with me me
no wan you to go.
When you no here, me long fa you
me goin' tell you so.
Stay wit me, forever now
me goin' make dis last.
Got no more time fa losin' you we
no goin' repeat de past.

So when did you become as cool as the night
with your every bare foot print?
Your mother must have known as I
that you were heaven sent.

Where are the bronze angels who brought you here
to this Caribbean Isle?
I'm sure the native girls just can't resist your
cool and sexy stylee.

Brother of the darkness
your arms as strong as elm.
the strength of them…just as sure
a completely mystic realm.
And in them…immediate solace;
A world I constant crave…
this dreadlock prince
of citrus scents
and most intriguing ways.

Brown-Sugared Babies

Wearing the nappy hair of my father
and the nose of the Ashanti—
for you
I'd have brown-sugared babies.

Broadcasting the cheek bones of my mother
and the temper of the Black Foot—
for you
I'd have brown-sugared babies.

Forsaking all others
and committing myself to you-
I'd have brown-sugared babies.

A Passionate Inheritance

(for my mother—the world's best "Mama")

I can't always contain this thing--
this passion that is yours...

though I can't honestly say that I try—
many days I'm nigh eruption
and your presence calms the raging sea.

Now that I have come of age
I realize that your peace is your strength
and I marvel at your ability to be so.

It drove me to Wilberforce you know
even though I'd never been away from home.
Such an exciting time for me,
and one that you said "kept you on your face."

I took it to Kenya with me
because it was one of my greatest companions.
It prompted me to serve diligently in the refugee camps
even though I'd been ganked for *six weeks* of clothes
and supplies in that lgarian Airport! Remember that?

If I remember correctly, you were presently on
your knees when you received
that bit of information.

I was led back home by it,
except now it looked similar to yours;

I was committed to a personal relationship with God

and to my innate ability to nurture and teach children

clearly the passion that is yours...
the same that kept you on your face
and can finally be seen in mine.

For Zoe

Oooh Baby, Oooooh Baby
Mama's got herself a chocolate Baby
And everybody wants the chocolate that she got
So they say…

Ooooh Mama Ooooh Mama
Just a little bit of your chocolate Mama
They begging me to share my chocolate but I'm not

For Saiwa

Cuddlebug and piggies everyday
Cuddlebug and piggies everyday

I would be like a ship without the sea
Without Cuddlebug and piggies everyday...
Hello piggy piggy

Natural Disaster

There is a force that drives the sane to insanity
the sensible to senselessness
the sighted to blindness
and it effortlessly confounds the wise.

It is the same force that brings hope to the hopeless
Strength to the faint
and energy to the listless.

So like sheep to the slaughter
We wade to it--as if we haven't known its pain.

Like deer, we pant for it--with every fiber of our beings
as if our very existence depended on it.

We have acquired a taste
for love's "sweet meat"
that oftentimes sours on our stomachs
and eventually burns like acid.
God help us as we reckon with this natural disaster.

A Manly Man

On a hot day
A cold day
A short day
A long day
The right day
The wrong day-I'll take a manly man.

Rough or rowdy
Spittin' or bawdy
Kinky hair-Oh Lawdy…A *manly* man.

An occasional unkempt nail is permissible you see-
that means he works well with his hands-
My Lawd he works well with his hands.

Be if far from me to deter him from growing that
five o'clock shadow-wherever it is…I will go.
Thank God for shadows…and *manly* men.

A Soulful Selection

Let me see your eyes
and I will read your song
they sing to me the song of your soul.
Your limbs may welcome passion
your lips may speak of hate
but your eyes…they play for me the song of your soul.

Be not quieted
let the chorus ring
the audience awaits your revue.

The seating is choice
the performance-preferred
we anxiously prepare for your news.

Sing oh choir of truths; drown not deception
the gawker deserves your best performance.

Allow the stringed instruments, their contribution
even if their selection brings mourning.

I Do Know It

I do know it.
I know what it looks like-
It looks like my dining room table today:

Places set, candle lit and a missing guest of honor.

It sounds like your fabricated excuses
as to why you couldn't be
where you were supposed to be
when your mouth said that you would be.

It smells like the scent that I unfortunately lifted from
your pillow cases last evening—
What brainiac ever thought to make lavender
the central ingredient in seemingly every cheap bottle of
eau de toilette?
That has got to be the most fabricated and disturbing
stench ever known to decent women!

It feels like this festering heartache
disguised as the swelling migraine
that is pulsing in the corners of my mind.

Oh yeah…I know it
and when I forget it, my senses remind me
and I remember again.

You, Everyday

Last night, I dreamed of quenching;
The desire for us was finally satisfied.
How saddened I was to be awakened.

Today, I envisioned my physical completion;
We walked seashore, side by side
and hand in hand
but truth only caused me pain

Tomorrow, I will attempt existence again.
The memories of such times are far gone.
Reality is a brutal punishment.

Rhapsody in Beautiful

Beauty is your cloak
Languid is your stride and beckoning shines
through the windows of your soul.

Merciful is your solicitation—
both timely and providential.

Copper Boy

I've never seen anyone like him-
The boy that bagged my groceries at the corner store.
And I just can't quite put my finger on what exactly-
in his cast
took captive my attention.

I'd say he was a "redbone," but that wouldn't suffice.
I'd say that he himself dripped from the honeycomb
 but that would only account for the overtones
through which the matrix of something exquisite

warm and radiant

permeated.

The most graduated sun
set in his face—just beyond the freckles
that were sporadically placed

in the most opportune spaces—
so that might account for the heat.

But somewhere between the graduated sun
and the honeycomb drippings

there must have been something else
responsible for that magnificent display...
What is that...clay?

Embarrassments?

Do say, do say.

Copper.
Burnished Copper; in all of its radiance
and all of its splendor.

He was gleaming copper
seeping through a garment of honey—undisturbed.

Community

Blacktopia

Blacktopia...

Where chocolate covered babies lay supinely
in the laps of their mothers
intoxicated from nature's libation
but keeping perfect time
with the rhythm of mother's heartbeat.

Blacktopia...

Where children frolic in waves of emerald pastures
while anxiously tumbling onto every
descending plateau;
they smear hands full of dirt onto their persons
for pleasure's sake.

Rolling with wild excitement where there might have
been paved roads
the sounds of their enchantment ride swelling vocal
chords
from the mouthpiece of each individual
temple of innocence.

Blacktopia...
Where my lover is decadent
He laces the night air with the scent of the sweetest loam
like the kind found on Alabama mounds
on Carolina foothills,
and in Mississippi mud.

He *is* the brother of darkness
and when he approaches
his very presence smothers all blinding light
and in his splendor
he hovers silently.
He hovers silently until former elements
have made adequate room for him.
Then...
from this daedalic device
trickles rivers of liquid gold- capable of producing nations—
oooh and it will
because here...love and music are one in the same
and its virtually impossible
to make one without making the other.

Blacktopia...
where every Friday night
there's a dance at the community center
and very old men jit till their pleading wives
convince them to "sit down!"

but their children laugh till salty tears
fall from their faces
and the grandbabies, who adore them,
scramble to keep up with them
atop the worn shuffleboard tiles

Blacktopia...
Where lazy hazy Saturdays
turn into backyard barbecues, card games, fish-frys
and a little bit of wine for "the heart's sake."

And while men take wine,
corn-row wearing princesses perfect the game of Double-Dutch
and little boys leave a trail of rainbow confetti
from punctured water bombs

Blacktopia...
Where the high–pitched laughter of women
floating on waves of cinnamon and ginger
from the opened kitchen window
reminds one listening lover of extraordinary
love making the night before.

So in the middle of the card game
He represses a newly-born desire by calling to her:
"Baby...y'all ain't finished that cake yet?"
His real motive being to catch a glimpse

of this face that will quench his unruly excitement-
at least till a more appropriate time arrives.

So over the stifling of congregated laughter
she answers:
"Yeah baby, we're comin' we're comin"
and the women burst into laughter again.

That'll Teach 'Em

That'll teach 'em Brown Sugar
that you ain't just bumpin' your gums,

when you finally tell that man—who ain't never meant you
no good...

Not only does NO mean NO, but next time baby...I ain't even
openin' the door.

That'll teach 'em Brown Sugar
that she mean what she say
when she looks that smug social worker square in the face
And say to her with conviction and with grace
Though I'm down today
It won't be long
'cause I been working out a plan
for me and my own.
When it's complete
you'll be the first to know
'cause it'll be a cold day in hell
'fore I dock at your door!

That'll teach 'em Brown sugar
that to fade us will be tough
when we invest in our children's survival
rather than True Religion, Prada and such.

That'll teach 'em Brown Sugar
that we've earned much respect
when thoughts of ourselves are
that we are better
and that we deserve the best.

We'll teach 'em Brown Sugar,
through your effort and mine.
It shall be accomplished;
This is our season
this is our time.

Brother Black

Brother Black, come back...
To arms that *can* hold you
To lips that *may* scold you
To legs that *will* wrap you
And to a heart that *does* love you.....*I* give *you* leverage.

Brother Black, come back...
To my arms because *I need you*
To my lips, *because* I read you
To my legs, *because* I crave you
To my heart, because *I* adore you...You *are* my leverage.

See, I have borne a nation in *your* honor.
Our children must have names
and *you* must name them.
As in the days of old, *you* must rear them.
Their heritage looks dim and *you* must show them.

We have managed to *look* like you...Our hair is tight.
We *talk* like you...Our rap is right.
We *love* like you...with all our might.
And we *move* like you from plight, to plight, to plight.

We are your reflection and we have need of you
She doesn't even know who you are.

Black is...

Black is...

...cornbread dressing, cornbread and corn fed, deep-
fried catfish all on the same plate.

... living from check to check but still finding
something *or somebody* to laugh at.

··· summertime family reunions and Blo(a)ck parties.

... Red Kool-Aid with enough sugar in it for a ten year kiss.

...four whole hours in the beauty shop chair while you
"low rate" your last hair dresser.

... your cousin Junebug an'em.

... the indelible memories of the Black glory days of
Afros, Cadillacs, Dashikis and Bell-bottoms.

... going to Sunday morning service --
every Sunday morning service at
the Second Ebenezer Missionary Baptist Church--
where the Right Reverend Dr. Cleophus Bullock is
"Passa."

... being able to successfully roll your eyes with *or*
without rolling your neck.

... double-starch creased blue jeans and a standing
appointment at the Mr. Johnson's Barber Shop.

... possessing a patent on an undeniably and intrinsically
poetic,
fluid, yet unforgiving...
"Kiss my motha' fu**in ass"
...So eloquent, so flawless; nah you know that's Black.

...arguing with your childhood friends about who got
the worst whippin'.

... realizing that by the time you make it half way
through the store, the security guard will more than
likely come back from his break.

... playing Double-Dutch in the middle of the street--on a
day so damn hot that *everybody's* seeing monkeys.

...going to "make" groceries, not *get* them.

... wondering how in the world did James and Florida
ever have a daughter that looked like Thelma.?

...Black eyed peas on New Year's Day, with a penny in
the pot for good luck.

Black is a cool Summer night with Frankie Beverly and Maze...
Ooooh yeah, now *that's* what Black is.

My Mama Didn't Raise No Bitches

You don't exist independent of me
And so therefore your actions *do* concern me
And furthermore they affect me

So when you cry, I cry
When you die, I die
When you laugh so heartily that salty tears run

down your cheeks, I want to taste just one of them.

You see, we are one in the same, so how dare you
violate this sacred temple by parading my body out to
savage, relentless, hungry paparazzi as if I was a load
of dirty laundry?
Why are you *uncovering* me instead of covering me?

How dare you sacrifice *my very honor* for a monetary
note that loses its value just a little more
each and every single day?

How dare you compromise my integrity as a prop in a
music extravaganza that is CLEARLY no more than a
15-second platform for fame
on the *New Millennium Minstrel Show*?

And who gave you the authority to change my name
without my mother's permission?

These Are My Sisters

These are my sisters--
All beautiful
All unique

Yet God has given us two things in common:
our magnificently rich culture and
His undying love for each and every one of us

Though our ancestors were taken from lands far far away
the benefits and wisdom that come to us
as a result of those passages
show through our actions
our motivations
and our self-determination.

Many prayers have pierced the atmosphere
on the behalf of my sisters and I,
and because of them,
we have no fear of the obstacles that lay before us;
but we approach them with tact,
with strategy,
with dignity,
and with the same wisdom
that has become our inheritance.

Therefore, we remain a thankful people.

We are thankful for many blessings.
We are thankful for much wisdom...
but most importantly...
we are thankful for our sisters.

The Celebration

Quiet yourself mother,
I hear you calling my name
Across the Atlantic Ocean
And over my amber waves of grain.
Daughter, Daughter
Come hither, and come quickly!
Then we can begin the celebration!

The sun rises high above Kilimanjaro,
And beckons for me at your command
Come, Come! He announces; Mother is calling
And we must begin the celebration!

I hear the rumble of the animals in the jungles.
They sense our excitement,
They share our anxiety too.

The monkeys have begun to groom each other
They too await our reunion.

The Acacia tree has stretched forth his arms to me
His is absolutely sure of my return.
Come sister! He says to me,
For the one who has given birth to us all
Is longing for her estranged children,
Make your way to us

And the stars will guide you by night.

For they have been instructed to wait on watch for you.

Let the young boys prepare to beat the drums of celebration
—my heart is in sync with their rhythm.
I will prepare for my voyage.
But quiet yourself mother Africa;
you contribute to my yearning,

Your cry has birthed my desires for home.

A Prayer for God's Displaced Children

Like precious and salvageable debris, they have been
gathered after a storm.

The children of mishap and circumstance have also
become prisoners of war.

A father –drinking
A mother –addicted,
A grandmother, unable to pay rent,
Has created a world of frenzy
for the victims of havoc's descent.

But this new "placement" promises safety-
A shelter to shield from their fears.
And though it's apparent, they'd choose to stay home-
They're coaxed, and even forced to adhere.

Who will hear the cry of the homeless?
The fatherless,
The motherless,
The child filled with loneliness and fright?

Who will stifle their pangs of anxiety,
or the emptiness that haunts them by night?
Oh God, let it not be the violator,
who robs them of child like faith...
Who soils their garments of innocence...
who forces emotional decay.
Him who defies the normalities of nature,
And trespasses a hideous sin,
on those whom God has deemed precious,
And those whose hearts He must now mend.

Lord stop the children's hearts from fainting,
while they await the unveiling of life's lot.
Allow them to bask in your loving kindness,
When circumstances prefer that they rot.

And send the angels to surround them
when they lay on these brand new beds.
Cut off the arm of the enemy,
Let the Lion embrace them instead.

Civil War

I woke up early on Tuesday morning
Seeing that my Philosophy class started at 9
and even though the clock struck as early as 6
The funky rhythm that is me
Beckoned for urban concoctions of
Hammond organ, Bass guitar
Rhodes piano and a tiggghhht tiggghht snare.

So darling, put the radio on
stereo but watch out for the
blows of:
Hos and gangstas, pussy and pimps
lickin and stickin bitches and chickens,

ballers and rims, fuckin--no lovin'
playas and niggas baby daddy's and jiggahs

blingin' and ridin' on spinners and chrome
ride and die chicks who got babies at home??
forreal? That's how you livin???

　　　While our babies are callin????
　　　While our babies are callin????

Y'all, while our babies are callin???
They are callin' for simple visions
of hope and peace.

Self-actualization is #5 y'all on the hierarchy of needs
So why are we still struggling with the basics and
returning on a *consistent* basis to former lessons learned?
Why are we still oblivious to *elementary* truths?????

Community Survival 101 is NOW IN SESSION!

"Keep a Livin Chile, Just Keep a Livin"

"You better watch you' mouth,"
that's what my Granny would say.

"You don't know why people do what they do-

all you can see is what *you* can see,
and only God's got a birds eye view."

"People runnin' round to and fro
'xaminin' the bidness of others-
and all the time, overlookin' they own,
and hopin' you don't look no futha"

"We knew a gal, with 15 chil'rin
wasn't married, lived 'round the way-
my uncle Jimmy bad mouthed dat po' chile,
sun up to sun down ev'ry day; He said,"
that gal ought to be whooped all dem chil'ren and no man-
she got to be de only woman I know 'round henh
that probly need to wear a pair of pants.

"Now Uncle Jimmy didn't know that gal had problems
her Paw made her play games she didn't wanna play-
and not soon enough
they hauled him off to jail
but why, she was too scared to say."

"Now Uncle Jimmy didn't know that gal had problems her
Paw made her play games she didn't wanna play- and not
soon enough
they hauled him off to jail
but why, she was too scared to say."

"Now my Uncle Jimmy's baby gal was sneeeeekay!

That gal was doin' mess he *never* knew-
that gal started havin' babies ev'ry year

Lawd, we thought ol' Jimmy would choke on his
chew."

"Keep a livin chile,' just keep a livin," that's
what my Granny would say.
But Ms. Mary Joe must've not been listening
'cause Granny said Mary Joeseph gossipped all day!

Chile did you see Wilbur?

I try to be as nice as I can.
I just waved when he passed my house- you
know Mrs. Wilbur got anotha' man. And
girl I called Sis. Grimes.
You know they 'bout to lose they house?

But don't let it be said I told ya dat
I said I'd be quiet as a mouse.

I was goin' by the school house on Thursday,
to get that recipe from Peggie Sue-
and don't you know I passed Minnie Lou's boy,
smokin' them funny cigarettes on Rte. 42?
Girl! I just try to mind my bidness.
and I know you do the same.
I just told you so you can pray
'cause I reckon they goin' insane.

Granny said, "Mary Joe could go on fa days

and I just let her go-

'cause I don warned her too many times;

gal yo gon' reap what you sow."

"But it wadn't long," Granny said,

"'fo de mess his de fan-

'cause on the front page of the Picayune Gazette,

was a pitcha of *Mary Jo's new man!*"

"Till den, nobody knowed she had one

since her husband ran de general sto'

and de chil'ren round the school house laughed a while

'bout how she somehow found room for just one mo'"

"Nah, I don't know who made that call,

But it sho was in bad taste

But I reckon it was de same one told her husband his
house was bein' robbed,

and he'd better get there and make haste!

You could hear Mr. Joesph cockin' dat rifle, soon
as he hung up de phone.

But I don't think he was nearly 'spectin
the surprise he met at home!

Po' Sis. Grimes had to move Mary Joe in
when Mr. Joseph put her out—

and de money she made, at her brand new job,
helped to make payments on de Grimes' house.

"But I reckon the worst," Granny said, "….musta been
when Wilber's wife called Mary Joe on de phone-
said she wadn't gonna' share her *second* man and Mary Joe
had better find her own!"

She Demands My Attention

Her nappy hair is unkept
her chocolate skin is smudged
with the residue of what might have been a red lollipop
or maybe those Flaming Hot Cheetos

Her eyelashes were constructed
from the feathers of a peacock--I'm sure

She peaks around the corner of Herrington Elementary--
she's not supposed to be here
but she's looking for someone...
me...
you...

She's not taking part in the playground games
she has more important things to ponder

Her hands are hidden and wrapped
inside of her torn shirt--she's not speaking
but she *is* calling to someone...
me...
you...

The Frankenstein Monster

Generation X???????
Why don't you try...

Generation :"headed for failure"
Generation: "hell in a hand basket"
Generation " robbin' and killin'/shootin' and lootin'"
Generation : "crackheads and dope dealers"
Generation : "X-rated EVERYTHING!"
Generation : "soon to be eXtinct!"
Generation : "eX-con!"
Generation : "Gang Banger!"
Generation : "Please eXcuse yourself out of my face, 'cause

I've got better things to to do, Generation!"

Yada, Yada, Yada, Yada....

Why don't you Generation Xplain to me what the hell
they're supposed to do with the legacy you left?

For Nostalgia's Sake

On Friday, January 12th, 8:30 A.M., 4TH FLOOR
MATERNITY WARD, RM 418, bed B,
Pontiac Osteopathic Hospital,
to Joyce Marie —
while Silas Brent played his last hand of Bid Whist—
a hazelnut colored bundle of vehement lungs
heralded her own arrival,
and Just in time for the REAL party.

Cousin CD's flawless helmet of Black glory:
A perfect addition to his formidable ensemble of
Polyester Freedom Bells and shiny Black leather.
An impeccable goatee encircled a boiling cauldron that spew his
Rhetoric in politic.
His rhetoric could singe the very kernel of every Disenfranchised
Disillusioned
Discontent
And absolutely *op*pressed or *de*pressed heart
in a surrounding 50 mile radius.

Daddy had a Silver Bullet:
A 1972 Cadillac Coupe de Ville
with a diamond in the back, sun-roofed top
We were diggin' in the scene with a gangsta lean-
woo woo...

It was the perfect chariot for our Saturday—
or Sunday drive.
Every other day it was G.M.C. Truck and Bus for him,
but on our day,
the heat rays rode the airways
right into the sun roofed top
The leather seats melted underneath my skinny legs
and we were breathin' soouuup.

"Ooh...mercy, mercy me..."
it was Mama, fanning herself in the heat-
and Marvin from the Deluxe 8-Track Deck.

then...
Parliament Funkadelic—barking like Dogs...
Earth, Wind and Fire—crooning like a *woman*...
Little Michael Jackson—pleading' like a *grown* man...
and Aretha Franklin,
wailing like a woman with a broken heart.

We could hardly wait till Friday!
Fish Fry and Bid Whist for them
meant we were up long enough to watch Good Times
House FULL!

People hollarin'...

    Give me a fish sandwich Joyce!

        Eloise, will you get that hollin baby!

Oooh, Mercy, Mercy meeee...

        Sing Marvin baby Sing!

    Aunt Magg says "Somebody check on the kids"

Nigga...nah you know you cheatin'!

    Hey Homeboy,
    Light some inscense and pass me dem papers!

People drinkin'

People laughin'

People dancin'

People cursin'

People jivin'

People lovin'

People livin'

People bein'

Bein' Black...bein' beautiful...and just bein'.

This Woman

This woman
She was both revered and full of wisdom
and from her womb had come
the most honorable and noble men and women.
Having come of age,
they prospered from the lessons she'd taught them.

Yet in her old age this old woman,
both wisdomed and radiant
lay still in a blood pool
Her silvery cotton diadem
was a sponge for its
slow removal from the ground
—a tragic and loathsome decay.

The lashes of her eyes peeled and her pupils still dilated
from a revelation that came too late.
—she was steeped in the crimson
tell-tale signs of colonial mayhem.

My Ma Wear Plenty a Hat

Quiet? You sassy wench!
I didn't ask how *you* felt-
I'll plug your mouth full of Georgia cotton,
if you don't keep your comments to yourself.

And get back to your quarters.
I want you working before the sun starts to bolster.
And you needn't be thinking that because I saw
you tonight-
that you'll be treated *any* better.

    I be needin' my breakfast Lettie.
    And my chilluns needs they suck.
    You gwine have to do better 'bout pulling you weight
    'round henh 'cause I reckon I don' had enough.

    What's that you say? You sassin' me?
    Woman I 'clare; I'll slap you blind.
    You might be *thankin'* you belong to Massa Tom,
    But in these henh quarters,Woman you is mine!

Lettie, when you finish the starching *and* ironing
I have something special for you to do.
Can you see where the back of my lilly white heels
have been rubbing up against my boots?
Well good, because I want you to scrub that for me,
and be sure to take your time-
Master Tom hates rough skin
so I know he'll be much obliged.

And be sure to feed the children,
they're growing up so fast and quick-
soon we'll have to send for one of *your*
younguns to fetch little Melanie's sticks.

I'm counting on you to polish the basins,
Master Randall's here from England you know?
He's got a new shipment of 500 new niggers!
We must make him sad to go.

Ma? You just gettin' in? It's time for bre'fast.
I think Paw is rightful sore.
He say you need a branch cross yo' back
'cause you don't cook 'round henh no more.

I tried to stop him-but he going to the grove

say you gwine cook and that's that.
I wanna tell him-but I don' know how-

that Ma wear a plenty a hat.

64

Empowerment

The Color Black

The undertaker wears it because it's definite
the business man because it's powerful.

The fashion models stalk the catwalk
Paris to Milan—flaunting it
It's sexy!
It's striking!
It's hot!

The "Big Three" engineer drapes his mind's most
excellent creations in it
because it's both stylish *and* poignant.

Well...*I* wear it because its strong...
I wear it because it's insoluble...
I wear it because it's my birthright and baby...
nobody
wears it better.

Inside Myself Today

Today I'm inside myself.

I hope I don't get beside myself.
I'm sure I don't appear to be myself.

But today, I can't carry anyone else,
I'm inside myself today.

And here –for my dreams—I count the costs
here for my failure—I cut the loss

options are pondered; ideas are tossed;
I'm inside myself today.

I'll take this time to create of myself
To think of myself
To question myself

To challenge the talents that lay dormant on my shelf;
I'm inside myself today.

I'll sing today...
I'll read today...
I'll paint today...
I'll write today...
I'll find a quiet place—for peace I'll pray.
I'm inside myself today.

I Too am Woman

Can't you see, that I too am a woman?
even though my plans I assert
even though I take what I want
even though I don't display hurt ?

Cant' you see that I too am a woman?
although I know I aggress
I take that bull by the horns
'cause I can't settle for less.

Can't you see that I too am female?
let alone my gifting to lead
put aside my ability to speak
cast away my desire to achieve.

Because you seem to have read me wrong
as if of the female gender I don't belong
like I couldn't possibly have a need to lean
especially since I don't *love* to clean.

Well I too need someone to watch for me
someone who's considerate enough
to hold the door for me;

but who isn't intimidated by *my* craving to acquire my
zest for life
and my right to aspire...

For femininity doesn't require
that I exhibit passive traits
in the eyes of the man that is sure of *his* fate.

In Pursuit of Success

How dare you hide your face from me…
Like a mischievous child
overindulging in a self-serving game of
hide and seek?

Ducking and dodging around corners,

Purposely giving only a glimpse of your splendor.

You have crouched behind obstacles,
Like a sniveling coward;
Letting off your sweet scent.
Only to gallop to your next destination,
When you've realized that I was aware of your location-

You knew that I was gaining on you.

Run. If you must.
But know that I will walk you down
Like the disease of cancer;

Devouring your *meat of necessity*.

If you make your bed in the mountains,
I will find you there.
If you sink to the deepest part of the ocean.
I will extract you.

You cannot elude me-
YOU WILL COME TO ME!

Niggas Niggas Niggas

I keep running into niggas that look like Brothers
Brothers please identify your selves…

Perhaps my faulted vision has contrived an obstruction
But Brothas, pleeeease identify yourselves

See, I can't always tell by the clothes that you wear

Niggas are wearin' locks like Ru Paul is wearing hair.

They're vibin' to Indie Arie
And sporting the ankh
They've pitched those plastic curl caps and

proclaiming:
Walaikum Assalam!

According to Brotha Malcolm, and brilliantly portrayed
by Denzel…

I've been hoodwinked, runamuck, bamboozled —
hell two or three niggas and you got a story to tell.
So…
Yea though I walk through the valley of the shadow of
death…
(huuuuuugh) let me catch my breath
aaaand clear my throat,
pitch my knife 'less I cut a throat—
Yeah…let me try to finish this rhyme on a lighter note:

Eeny meeny miiny moe
Catch a nigga by his toe
If he hollar Choke him mo'
Cause niggas be slippin',
                flippin
                trippin',
                dippin'
                dippin
                dippin...

their *God's gift to women* in any random *ho*
And all the time they beggin' for committment

And smilin' like angels
when they're bonified hell sent

and singin...'
                Won't you be...
                won't you please...
                please won't you be my...

                Lover of a million nights
                Keeper of a thousand dreams
                My ray of hope in most dismal scenes-

Butter from that nigga's tongue had me
trippin' like one of Solomon's fiends.

So in the event that our paths should cross,

I humbly implore all imposters to quietly pass on the left

Because if I run into another nigga
Spittin' his game with finesse and rigor
I'm gonna be forced to pull a trigger
and have him stuttering like Tigger
If I run into another Nigga!

Disgruntled Domestic

I'm not crazy about cooking,
And I wish I could find someone to help me clean-
I'd have trouble mending a hole in my sock,
I fight with the washing machine.

The grocery store makes me nervous,
And I hate sewing patches and quilts-
I'd love having children...but not at this point,
So even the thought gives me chills.

But who said I had to be domestic?
Ooh, if I could just get my hands around his throat!
'Cause I've been expected to function this way-
since my mothers were dragged from the boat!

Well guess what...My name ain't "Mammy"
And though her place was important for me-
I choose to multiply the fruit of her labor, I'm
workin' on another degree.

My Sister's Attic

In my sister's attic is a collection of things-
And here, these things have found a place for rest.
Some of them are valuable, but most of them are not-
Yet for them all, she has somehow found a place.

The box on which the sky light casts a shadow-
Is another that she would never display for view.
For in it, she has placed the stench of lonely-
At one time her arms held a lover too.

The heaviest of the crates, is on the table-
She has managed to fill it with weary thoughts.
Her plan has been to keep this crate well hidden
For she must stay afloat, weary or not.

This is not a place for folly, as in the days of old-
The children cannot come here to play.
Lest they find her packaged *disenchantment*-
She never thought her life would read this way.

Items large and small, have been placed here-
for safe keeping;
Some she's brought alone,
while others she has needed help to bring.

But more importantly, she has guarded them-
So many times, by others they weren't seen.

In the corner, she has placed a small container.
In this container she laid away a scar.
Though the scar is small, it has maimed her.
Her father is to blame, he lived afar.

But there's a larger chest beside the mirror-
Inside are family heirlooms -hers by rite.
With brilliance as of diamonds lay **resilience!**
The same that aided slaves both day and night.

Longevity is neatly packed beside it-
Like fine linen, **strength** lines the inner floor.
Many know not of my sister's attic-
But the contents of this chest, won't be ignored.

There's No Wonder...

No wonder they want to kill him.
He was the first man to ever talk with God.

No wonder they want to kill him,
He was responsible for the erection of the Egyptian
pyramids.

No wonder they want to kill him,
He performed the first open heart surgery...
But they haven't been able to kill him,
For his spirit won't let him die.

I won't kill him either,
By telling him that he can't provide.
I won't kill him either,
By saying that he won't amount to anything.

I won't kill him either,
By saying that he doesn't deserve respect.
I will protect him from those who are out to take his life
He is necessary for my survival...

and so I will encourage him

I will brace him

I will love him.

13 Ways of Looking at the Black Woman

I

After eons of systematic degradation and the attempt of
annihilation by an entire country against
her…remaining constant is the Black woman.

II

You can hear her praises on the lips of the children-

not just her children-most children, for she in some
capacity has cared for them all… the Black woman is
steeped in the ability to nurture.

III

Eve is the Black woman.

Eve is the African woman. Eve
is the mother of all living.

IV

If the sea of humanity stood hand in hand and side by side,

not even her coif would let her be just typical.

V

There have been attempts at many things:
walking the moon,
building the airplane, etc.
but who can attempt being the Black woman?
Certainly not Ru Paul.

VI

The Black woman
Perseverance

Fortitude

Strategy

Wisdom

Love
as well as hips, attitude and big lips

VII
What the Black woman is not-is sex.

Though massa took it-

The slave brother learned to loathe it-

The 70's used film to exploit it –
and new millennium hip hop does the same;
Yes, she is sexy –
she is not sex.

VIII
Never ending jobs belong to the Black woman
The butcher, the baker, the candlestick maker?

The PROVIDER

The TEACHER

The LOVER

The SPIRITUAL LEADER

The BANKER

The STUDENT

and employee #821 on the Daimler-Chrysler line. IX

The automobile

Mt. Everest

Facebook

The Black woman

X

When America said that nappy hair was hideous-

The Black woman developed a hot-comb to change it.

When the Black woman realized

that America doesn't define the Black woman-

The Black woman pitched that hot-comb

in the garbage can.

XI

1st...beautiful Black baby girl

2nd...Black, baby girl who painfully learns the

dehumanizing strategies of this society.

3rd...resisted Black girl (especially if she's dark skinned)

4th... hopefully...a proud Black woman.

XII

Black woman: the 8th Wonder of the World!

XIII

The Blacker the woman…the sweeter the wisdom.

Musings

The Fabric of Me

I am gold and marigolds
Oranges and mango
a five o'clock flower on the southern eve

I am urban skyscrapers kissing smoky indigo skies
and this is the fabric of me:

Window boxes filled w/crimson stained pansies
Juxtaposing cold and gray stoned stoops
The night fall pregnant with smells from love's kitchen
Badoo da dii daaa dii da doooo.....

Explosions of funky rhythms
pulsating on the downbeat
onto air stagnant backstreets
You can't beat this kind of heat
                    not even with a stick
So breathe black people...
go on and breathe
cause Funk is **hot**
Rhythm is demanding and I...am in the making.

Arima

The skies are alive with sunshine,
and the streets with the business of the day.
Look how the *pothounds lime* in the road,
While the children continue their play.

The vendor's *roti* fills up the traveler,
and the *fruit of the cashew* subdues.
The *coconut water* refreshes him,
the juice of the *Mango* does too.

Embrace the humid density,
the mist from the ocean's tide-
feel the pineapple's outer shell,
reminiscences of the porcupine.

Smell the incense of the *Rastaman*

and the Hibiscus on the hill-
discern the citrus, as it seeps through the rain,
with hints of banana still.

Listen to the *Reggae* from the *bungalows,*
and hear the ocean's song.
Of innumerable places, one might reside,
it's most for Arima I long.

Amina's Eyes

"Nabat"
She said, when she touched my hand
I was quite surprised that she had.
Somali children didn't come this close
Not even for the food in my bag.

I stretched out my hand to touch her,
But she quickly found cover to hide-
And never a vision, have I witnessed-more
pure Than Amina's dancing eyes.

Leisure

I understand that First Lady Obama
might enjoy a game of golf

and Oprah Winfrey, the talk show host
might get "on mark" for take off

Patricia McCloud, the lecturer
might tour Francisco Bay

with less to do, I'm privy to
a muggy day and Reggae.

...On Being Transparent

For as long as I can remember
it has never been in my best interest
to be completely honest with any man
because being so has never caused a single one of them
to alter the way that he has interacted with me
upon having received that information.

Now that I think about it-

for as long as I can remember
I can't think of any man
who's been completely honest with me.

Speakeasy

I done heard mo' people talk about how they don't thank Negroes ought to use bad anglish but I won't repeat none of it 'cause I don't thank its worf repeatin' I mean, I see it like this: African-Americans are phonetic geniuses- Just think about it, what other language changes as rapidly and as often as the particular form of English that's spoken by African-American, while still retaining a common understanding among its members...Well? Yet this ever-evolving, somewhat tribally universal language isn't taught in schools but is somehow passed to each generation with full, solid understanding??? Check it, Yo. Sistahs and Brothas be spitting MAD creative game *everywhere*, especially when we flow/So ... if the *man* don't wanna peep that a give up some props, then later for that Yo, 'cause each one gotta teach one kidd and I can't spend my time tryin' to convince you or him of a smothered truth that *he* really peeped like....yesterday; Deuces!

For Carnell,

(who went to that gig that he didn't tell us about)

Carnell,

I'm leaving this note for you, since I didn't catch you before you left for your rehearsal. Why didn't you tell us about this one You usually tell us about all your gigs, I guess you wanted to do this one solo.

I was tellin' Garard the other day how awesome it is that God put all three of us in the same family. We really have a lot to be thankful for –I mean, you might find one or two talented people in the same family but you don't often find all siblings being musically inclined and their talents complementing each other You know what else is funny? That Bishop Warren made you play, and made me sing, and made Garard "beat them drums" when we were kids. Who would have known that we would have grown up to work together so very well? I guess he knew what we didn't; you know they did say he was a Prophet.

Anyway, here's the point: we gotta get on them songs. I do miss you being at New Jerusalem 'cause it ain't as easy as it used to be to get together for practice but that shouldn't stop us from doing what God has given us to do as a family, you know? Plus I have classes, Garard has classes and work and I know you have your Berea rehearsals with the Praise team too, but somehow we're gonna have to make time.

Well I'll talk more about it with you later – especially since I said I was only leaving you

a note (smile).

Love Ya, Sis

P.S.
I can't believe you didn't tell us about this rehearsal. You didn't even put it on your calendar.

If I Had Time

If I had time,
I would clean that corner in the crack,
roud the back of my bedroom door--
it irrates me every time I'm forced to look in that direction

If I had time, I'd organize my closets to perfection:
overcoats, light jackets, sweaters then blouses and shirts
long dresses, short dresses, slacks and then skirts--
damn...I gotta get me some time

If I had time, I might push "rewind"
and watch Scandal for a second or *maybe even* a third time
that Jake knows he is FINE...but I ain't got no time

If I had time, I would set the clocks back
for the Spirit of Detroit
to a time when the Cadillac was King
a Coney Island was supreme
and if you really wanted to see BLING
then a Friday night cruise
on Jefferson Ave. was just the thing...
man, where did the time go?

If I had time, I'd mail all those letters
I'd swap out those blinds
Id call my cousin in Texas
I'd wrap Fammy's newspapers in twine

Damn if I had time, I'd finish this rhyme.
to be continued...

Sibling Muse

You were my muse;
Ever since sixth grade you were.

I didn't know that I would be a total disaster at playing the
clarinet;

I only knew that I wanted to experience the satisfaction that
you did when you reigned majestically in the first chair of
the cornet section of the Mighty Chiefs Marching Band -
Pontiac Central was glad to know you.

Luckily, it didn't cost Momma and Daddy more
than the $300 that they gave Grinelle's for that
clarinet, before we *all* realized the mistake.

But my idolizing you and your art is what led me to me and
mine

Because after my collision with Performance Band,
I wandered aimlessly into the Bulwark that is me.

Eventually I found the same relationship with
Ms.Phillips and Mr. Krontz
That you'd developed with "Cool ass Mr. Wise"

Sometimes my play rehearsals lasted as long as your band
rehearsals –I really thought I was doin' somethin' then...

So you've been my muse...just as you are now
But I sing, write and create, simply because you were.

Death is No Gentleman

On yesterday, he descended mightily
with vengeance on Columbine High-unexpected,

Unexplained and definitely uninvited.
Yet he walked coolly through the entrance
doors of the cafeteria and the library

as if permissioned to cancel the appointments
of those who refuged there...such a violation.

On Monday he sneaked into Carnell's apartment-
unexpected,
unexplained and again uninvited.
He didn't know or announce himself.

He didn't even have the decency to call before he came;
he simply walked through the front door
up the stairwell

and climbed into bed with him –just as he did Daddy's
such indecency.

Cry at birth?

Rejoice in death?

How, when it is so indecent?

How, when it is so untimely?

when it is so uncompromising and conclusive?

It simply has no manners;

death is no gentleman.

I'm Really "Doin' Good"

He says he's proud of me:
Here I am 29 years old,
Been fired from my permanent job,

Living at home with Mama,
on a bachelor's degree that I can't use,

And scufflin' with the creditors,
so I can go back to school and work on anther one.

I have nothing in my name, save my car—and
that's only till I'm late on a payment…but
he says to me:

> "Vick, somebody asked me the other day how
> you were doin'",
>
> I said: she's doin' good.
> She's workin' on getting back in school,
> Workin' on her books; copyrighting her songs.
>
> She's teachin' now —at school and church-
> She travels internationally-
> And she don't have no unwanted babies!
> Yep. She's really doin' good.
> And I'm proud of you Sis, I'm really proud."

So I said:
"I'm really doin' good."

Where I Abide

The lone flicker of a candle's light
shed the scent of cosmetic vanilla beans—
hardly the real thing but surprisingly pleasant.
It illuminates a small space in this area of this room.

An old antiqued oak night stand,
complete with cup rings
and sharp art-decorated edges
supports the most necessities:
an incredibly temperamental alarm clock
a box of Indian incense
and a Photographer's box of Trojan condoms
because Costco had a sale
and the days of *frequent Friday rendezvous*
aren't so frequent as of late.

Somewhere beneath the massive down-filled leopard
print comforter is a full sized bed
and a pair of my black panty hose—or were they blue?

The sand colored carpet is still new in most places
but is a testament to my daily adventures.

A beaten path that rightly accommodates an
8 1/2 women's regular
leads directly to the bathroom
and the front door... I love this place

In just moments I will pour--in this place
a glass of the darkest Merlot I could find
Then I'll step into a cauldron of water equipped
with Egyptian Musk oil
and bubbles as big as snowballs.
Finally...I'll welcome the regulars into this place...

    Welcome Jilly from Philly
    Come on in Indie

    Muuuuuusiiiiiq!

    My man KEM!
    Raheem, I'm glad you could make it
    Dwele and the BBC?
    Ya'll know Motown is ALWAYS welcomed.